In memory of
Justin Mowrey
(4/12/90 - 6/30/20)
(Fran Mowrey's son
who found Molly)
&
Martin Berger
(9/20/42 - 5/31/14)
(father of Frances Mowrey)
He was at the
Mowrey home
on this unforgettable day!

All rights reserved. No part of this book may be reproduced or transmitted in any form or by any means, electronic or mechanical, including photocopying, recording, or by any information storage and retrieval system, without permission in writing from the copyright owner. The views expressed in this work are solely those of the author and do not necessarily reflect the views of the publisher, and the publisher hereby disclaims any responsibility for them.

Copyright © 2020-2022 * Higgins Publishing. All rights reserved. Michelle Larson * Molly's Thanksgiving Adventure

Higgins Publishing supports the rights to free expression and the value of copyright. The purpose of copyright is to encourage writers and artists to produce creative works that enrich our values. The scanning, uploading, and distribution of this book without the express permission of the publisher is a theft of intellectual property. If you would like permission to use material from this book (other than for review purposes), please contact permissions@higginspublishing.com. Thank you for your support of copyright law.

Higgins Publishing | www.higginspublishing.com - The publisher is not responsible for websites (or their content) that are not owned by the publisher. Higgins Publishing is committed to excellence in the publishing industry. The company reflects the philosophy established by the founder, based on Psalm 68:11, 'The Lord gave the word, and great was the company of those who published it.'

Library of Congress Control Number 2020912173

Larson, Michelle
Molly's Thanksgiving Adventure
ISBN 978-1-941580-91-2 (HB) * 978-1-941580-41-7 (PB) * 978-1-941580-92-9 (EB)
November 2020

For information about special discounts for bulk purchases, subsidiary, foreign, and translations rights, contact Higgins Publishing at sales@higginspublishing.com.

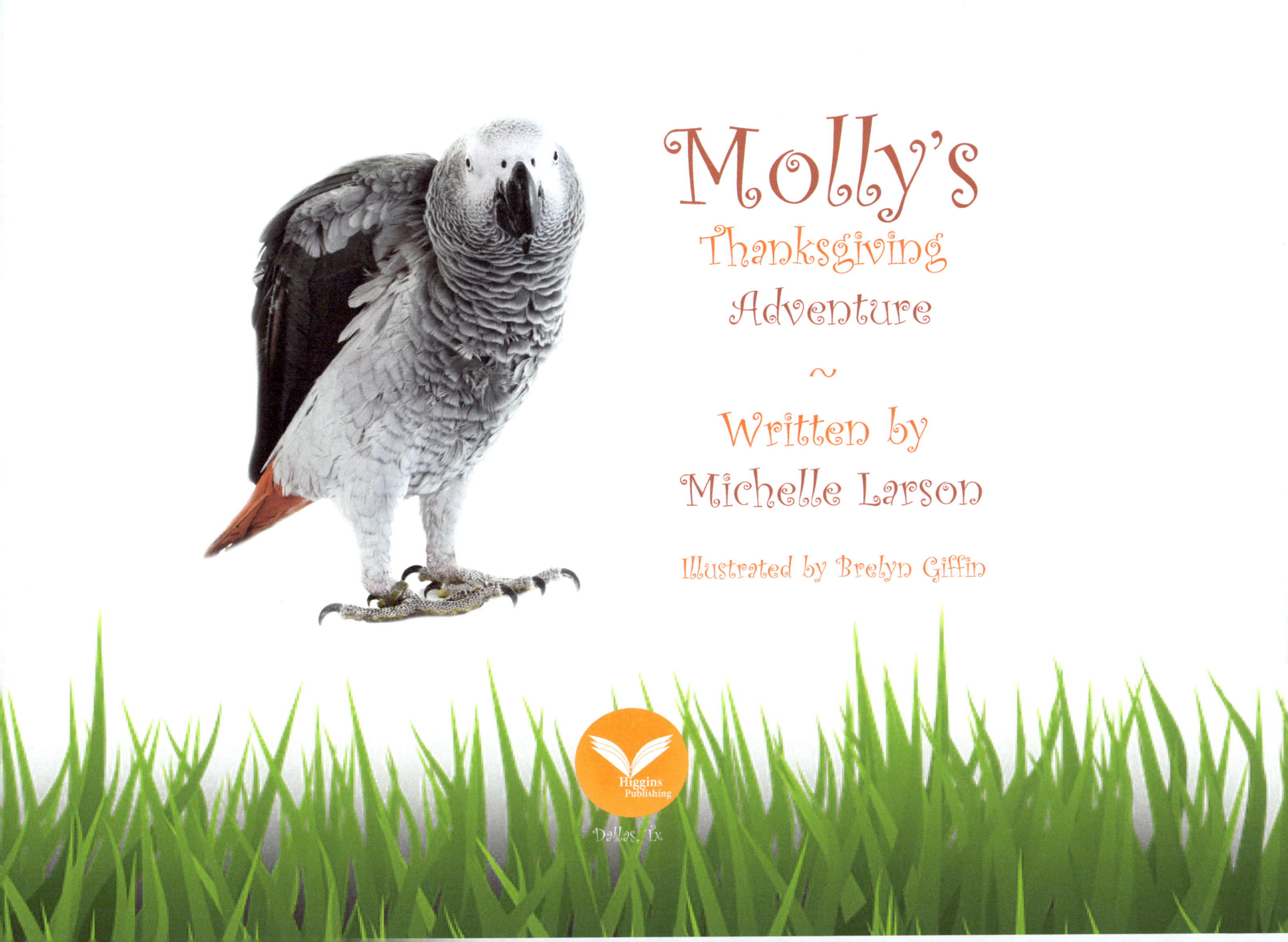

Molly's
Thanksgiving Adventure

~

Written by
Michelle Larson

Illustrated by Brelyn Giffin

Higgins Publishing

Dallas, Tx

It was time for a gathering
as everyone made their way,
To the Mowrey home that Thanksgiving Day.

It was hustle and bustle,
people in and out the door,
However, no one had a clue as to what was in store.

Little did 'Mama' or anyone else know,
That Molly the bird was watching
The door open to and fro.

She was imagining what the real world outside was like,
'That looks fun,' Molly thought,
as she saw a boy riding a bike.

Then the moment came when the door was left ajar,
Molly seized the opportunity
and her wings moved her very far.

Up, up and away, over the trees and into the sky,
She barely looked back to wave goodbye.

Now everyone was running around frantically aware,
That Molly was now 'somewhere out there!'

One thing for sure, dinner would have to wait,
as we scoured the area,
hoping to save Molly from a terrible fate.

We looked by the school,
the ball field, the bushes—where could she be?
And then, 'Is that you Molly way up high in that tree?'

Why, yes it was—Yay!! We found her at last!
But, then, 'Oh no!'
She got scared and took off very fast!

'How did it happen?
We lost her once again,'
Now the night would pass
without Molly in her pen.

No one slept well that night
as we were all feeling rather sad,
'It got so cold last night!
Is Molly ok? If so, is she mad?'

One thing was sure, we weren't giving up hope!
There had to be a way,
We were determined to find Molly
and bring her home that day!

Searching and searching,
in scary and jagged places, all over the land,
Even the neighbors pitched in
and lent a helping hand.

As our hopes of finding her and that she made it
through the night began to fade,
Everyone took some time to bow down,
and oh how we prayed!

We started to pass out flyers and continue to search;
things were all abuzz!
But wait, what was that over there on the ground?
Why yes—it was!

Justin had found Molly sitting in a backyard,
alive and well,
Boy, now we all have quite a story to tell.

About that very memorable Thanksgiving Day,
When Molly decided to celebrate
in her very own special way!

Molly's Personality

Molly loved to talk and say hello, imitating family member voices and make backing up beep sounds. One of Molly's favorite sayings was "Molly a good girl" and making kissing sounds.

Molly loved to dance to music and bob her head, making snapping sounds to a beat. She also loved popcorn, peanuts and anything sweet. Sadly, Molly left us in June 2019 at the age of 21. We will always remember this adventure.

ABOUT THE AUTHOR

Michelle Larson resides in the Houston, Texas area, along with her two pre-teen sons. Originally hailing from the small town of Lewistown, PA, Michelle's family members have always been animal lovers, which is evident in her passionate writing about how pets are truly a part of the family.

Having personally written poems over the past 30 years, Michelle has now expanded her writing skills to move into the Children's' Book arena. She plans to author several more books to showcase her originality and creativity and to further display her passion for animals.

Michelle hopes that she can bring enjoyment and fun into the lives of children worldwide as they learn to read and interpret stories, getting them excited to turn the pages.

When not writing or working as an Instructional Designer, Michelle enjoys spending time with her boys, traveling, hanging at the beach, or bike riding. After reading her book, you will understand why "Fun" is her middle name and why she incorporates laughter into her daily life.

www.ingramcontent.com/pod-product-compliance
Lightning Source LLC
Chambersburg PA
CBHW041915230426

43673CB00016B/418